Christmas Memories of Mr. and Mrs. Santa Claus

CHARLIE JONES

SEVEN LOCKS PRESS

Santa Ana, California

Seven Locks Press
P.O. Box 25689
Santa Ana, CA 92799
(800) 354-5348

Individual Sales. This book is available through most bookstores or can be ordered directly from Seven Locks Press at the address above.

Quantity Sales. Special discounts are available on quantity purchases by corporations, associations, and others. For details, contact the "Special Sales Department" at the publisher's address above.

Printed in the United States of America

Library of Congress Cataloging-in-Publication Data
is available from the publisher
ISBN 1-931643-99-7

Cover and interior design by Heather Buchman
Front cover: "Santa's Approval"
Model: Santa Cliff
Artist: Ralph J. McDonald
Photographer: Tim Talley
Back cover: "Santa Charlie"
Photographer: Kim Doren

*D*edicated to all the Santas, St. Nicks, Kris Kringles, Father Christmases, Pere Noels (French), Sinterklaas (Dutch), Jultomtens (Sweden), Babadimris (Albania), Babbo Natales (Italy), Papa Noels (Mexico), Kaledu Senelis (Lithuania), and Weihnachtsmanns (Germany) throughout the world. And especially to Santa Joe, Santa@KringleEnterprises .com, who climbed into his sleigh a little early in the year, to lead us on this great adventure.

Introduction

Creating *Christmas Memories of Mr. and Mrs. Santa Claus* was the most fun I've had since Christmas morning when I was in the fourth grade. Leaning against our big, fat, decorated Christmas tree, with my name on it, from Santa, was a beautiful, brightly shining, silver color, aluminum bicycle. It was probably the last aluminum bicycle manufactured until after World War II. In addition, it was the lightest, fastest, bicycle in Rogers School. I won all the races for the next three years. Lance Armstrong had nothing on me.

— Merry Christmas, Charlie Jones

Table of Contents

Finding Santa

If you ask a group of first- or second-graders what they want to be when they grow up, you will get myriad answers. Kids want to be firefighters, policemen, teachers, astronauts, movie stars, TV stars, sports stars, Bill Gates.

One occupation you never hear is Santa Claus. Santa is too big, too magical, too wonderful to even be thought of as a career. You have to work all year 'round creating all those toys, and it's COLD living at the North Pole. Besides, every kid knows there is only one true Santa, and the big guy himself already has that job.

So how does one become Santa? What makes a perfectly sane man grow a long beard, don a red suit, and invite children and sometimes adults to sit on his lap and tell him their most intimate wishes? SSHHHH, I'm going to let you in on Santa's personal secret. This is a secret that only the men in the red suit know. Here it is: You don't find Santa. Santa finds you.

One day you look in the mirror and the red beard you've sported most of your adult life is no longer red. As much as you try to keep it neatly trimmed to make people think you are Sean Connery, your general body build always gives you away. As hefty as Kenny Rogers is, he still has more hair than you, and Burt Reynolds can afford a much better toupee than you can.

Kids start asking, "Are you him?" And soon adults do, too. You start to prefer red jackets, shirts, and ball caps, and you're not even an Arkansas Razorback fan. ("Go Hogs!!!") Then one day you walk into a salon and Santa walks out. How did you get to this point?

Every professional Santa I know has had a defining moment. Something theologians call an "aha" experience or an epiphany. It's that moment when doubt ceases and faith begins. You no longer think you *may* be a good Santa, you know with every cell of your being that you *are* Santa. Mine goes like this:

I had been driving a school bus for three years, having decided that I really liked working with kids more than I wanted to manage people. I had worked my way up to a countywide standby position and had become the night dispatcher for the twenty-fourth largest school bus fleet in the nation. In short, I was a problem solver and the "go to" guy.

It was the last day of school before the Christmas break, and I had been assigned to an elementary school where I had never driven before. It's been my habit to wear a red and white Santa's stocking cap around the holidays, and I decided to wear one that afternoon. I thought it might be fun to have "Santa" drive the kids. Trust me, I was completely unprepared for what happened next.

As the younger kids boarded first, most were totally stunned. In their regular driver's place was a big guy with a real gray beard, wearing a red jacket and a Santa cap, the day before Christmas break!

Some of them asked in quiet voices full of awe, "Are you really here?" "I can't believe it!" "Are you him?" I told them I was and that their parents had asked me to check on them to make sure they were really being good.

As the upper grades boarded, they were skeptical but seeing the reaction of the younger students, decided it would be okay to play along.

I don't know how long it's been since you've been on a school bus but I can tell you it's a noisy, rowdy place. This is especially true if you are a substitute driver. That day, you could hear a pin drop.

It was the best school bus ride I ever had! Not a single kid misbehaved. The magic of Christmas had found my school bus on a cold afternoon in December, AND Santa had found me.

— SANTA JAC, RBS, BSC*

* Real Bearded Santa, Bachelor of Santa Claus

Trial Run

My first time as Santa was at the Christmas party that I host for my friends and church family. I thought I would try out being Santa at home first, to see how it went.

I had a bag of toys for the kids and in my bag, I also had a Collectible Porcelain Barbie Bell. Every time one of the boys would jokingly complain, I offered to swap him the Barbie. This always drew laughs.

Just as I was leaving, a little three-year-old girl tugged on my pant leg. I bent down to hear what she was saying. She whispered, "When you come to my house for your *real* visit, may I please have a Barbie?"

Well, I reached into my bag and pulled out the Collectible Porcelain Barbie Bell. When I handed it to her, her eyes were as big as saucers. I said, "All you had to do was ask."

After leaving, with a lot of, "Ho, Ho, Hos," I went around the house into the garage, quickly changed my clothes, and returned. When I entered, she came over to me and proudly held the Barbie Bell up real high, shook it, made it ring, and said, "Look what Santa gave me."

(THERE IS STILL MORE)

My First Real Visit

My home party was just a TRIAL RUN for what I had already planned, which was a visit to a local hospital to make the rounds of the kids' wing.

One of the youngsters in the hospital that night was a mentally handicapped blind girl. She was twelve years old but I was told by her parents that in her mental state, she was more like a baby.

I asked them if I could give her a toy and they thought maybe a stuffed animal made of different textures would be appropriate, so that she could feel it. I reached into my Santa's bag and pulled out a Teddy Bear made of different types of materials.

I placed it in her hands, but this did not make her happy at all. She just pushed it away. I tried several times, but she kept pushing the Teddy Bear away. She was not pleased with my gift.

I playfully stomped my foot in mock frustration. The bells on my boots gave out a ring, and she immediately squealed with delight. I was trying to figure out what made her so happy, then I moved, the bells rang, and she giggled again with great delight.

Then we all knew. So I shook one boot and she giggled. Then I shook the other boot and I was rewarded again with that most charming giggle.

The rest of the time as I stood there talking with her parents, I was shaking one boot or the other. Every jingle of the bells was met with a charming giggle from that beautiful little girl. I felt like it was really Christmas.

Jingle-Jingle / Giggle-Giggle,

Jingle-Jingle / Giggle-Giggle,

Jingle-Jingle / Giggle-Giggle.

For the first time in my life, I felt I was really Santa Claus.

— SANTA JEFF

SANTA BULLETIN: If you want to become one of Santa's helpers, you can enroll for your HED (Honorary Elf Diploma). You can even e-mail a photo of your personalized diploma to all your friends. If you're interested, check your SATs (Santa's Absolute Thoughtfulness) to see if you qualify. Then go online and check into the ELF SCHOOL.™ The rest is up to you and Santa.

Santa's Mission

My Dad loved Christmas! It was his favorite time of the year. He loved the music and the Christmas carols and the lights and the food and decorating the house for the holidays. We didn't have a big house, so there wasn't a lot of decorating.

Every year Dad would have a Christmas photo taken that he would print at his shop for the family. I remember our friends would be so impressed to receive a customized Christmas card. This was before color cards and photo cards became popular.

I remember one card that was a photo of my brother and me sitting in front of our fireplace with a plastic Santa Claus between us.

On Labor Day weekend of 1962, my Dad and his brother made a trip to Camp Lejune Marine Base to pick up his brother's two sons who had just gotten out of the Marine Corps.

I remember Dad talking to me the morning before he left about how he didn't really want to be gone for the holiday weekend, but his brother wanted him to ride along.

Dad couldn't drive, but he felt he could at least keep his brother company. So, with reluctance, he bid us good-bye. That was the last time I saw him. On the return trip, all four were killed in a head-on collision when a truck hit them after passing another vehicle.

I wasn't able to see him again because they all had closed casket funerals due to the severity of the injuries. My childhood ended on that Labor Day weekend as I realized I was the man of the house.

As Christmas came around that year, my Methodist Youth Fellowship group decided to provide a Christmas party for a mission church in our town, and they asked for a volunteer to be Santa Claus. People had always made fun of me for being overweight, so I was elected to be Santa.

Deep down, though, I felt the fake beard and red suit would cover up the hurting person inside. If I could bring happiness to others, then maybe that would ease the loneliness from which I was aching.

So, for Christmas of 1962, I put on my first Santa Claus suit and made my "grand entrance" at the Beddington Street Mission in High Point, North Carolina, carrying a hand-cut cedar Christmas tree on my back and a big bag of toys for the children.

The rest of the members of the youth group followed and with the children, we made construction paper link chains to decorate the tree. Santa passed out presents to all the children while the other youth group members served refreshments. Little did I know that qualifying to be Santa because of my size was the beginning of a life-long ministry.

I had been given a mission for my life, even though I didn't realize it at the time. In the process, God had chosen a most unlikely person to be HIS messenger of unconditional love and acceptance through a fat kid dressed up as Santa Claus.

God had chosen, just like He did in the Bible, a common, ordinary person to do an extraordinary job. Accepting the challenge and the mission was going to be up to me.

— SANTA CLIFF

A Brand New Santa

In my late forties, when my beard had whitened and I'd put on a little weight—okay, a lot of weight— my pastor said he might want me to be Santa the next Christmas.

The thought of having grubby kids climbing all over me prompted me to lose thirty pounds and trim my beard really close. Obviously, this wasn't the beginning of my Santa venture, but it was the first time it crossed my mind.

My true Santa venture started a few years later in early spring in a health food store. This was during a period in my life where I was beginning to consider what I might do in retirement. I was hoping that event would come about the time I turned sixty.

As I was chatting with the counter lady, she said, "You know, if you let your beard grow longer, you could play Santa Claus. I have a friend who makes as much money in six weeks playing Santa as I do all year." Now that was worth considering.

Over the next few weeks and months, a number of events guided my thinking. First, one source of my steady income became threatened and I began looking into the financial rewards of being Santa. Second, my exploration into Christian education generated the sound of one hand clapping in the forest, when you are all alone.

But then I was awarded with a license to hunt alligators. My daughter Katie, attending Bryn Mawr, would lay on a heavy southern accent and tell her fellow students, "My daddy's puttin' me through college by being an alligator hunter down in Florida!"

Then I signed up with a modeling agency, hoping to find work posing as Santa. You know the drill: You pay them money, they don't find you work. That's when Katie told all her friends, "My daddy put me through college by huntin' alligators, and now he's puttin' my brother through college by being a male model!" No work, but lots of laughs!

Later that year, I discovered the Charles W. Howard Santa Claus School, the oldest in America. What a wonderful experience. I learned the craft of being Santa Claus. The first lesson is, when you put on that red suit, you are not playing Santa Claus, you ARE Santa Claus.

I called my wife during one of our breaks and she asked if I was having a good time. I replied, "I'm sitting in a room with sixty Santas, wannabe Santas, and Mrs. Santa Clauses; I can't help but have a good time." And I was.

One day we piled onto the school bus to visit Bronners, the biggest Christmas store in the world. We were all wearing red sweatshirts with an embroidered outline of Santa and "I believe" stitched above, a gift from the school. We were also given cards printed with "I met Santa" to give to any children who might spot us in the store.

As I was wandering around wide-eyed in this huge emporium filled with every imaginable Christmas item, a young boy about five noticed my white beard and hair, so I smiled and waved. He stopped, put his hands on his hips, and said, "Are you the REAL Santa?"

I squatted down, and not having a response, I mumbled something. He suddenly lit up and gasped, "You ARE the real Santa! You brought me the Spiderman gloves last year!"

Quickly remembering his Santa manners he helped his younger sister from her stroller and brought her to me, saying, "This is my sister Autumn and I'm Oscar." I gave each of them a card and explained what it said.

Then I had my first magical moment talking about what they wanted for Christmas and reminding them to remember Rudolph and the reindeer when they left milk and cookies for Santa on Christmas Eve.

As I was telling them to be a good boy and girl, being somewhat flustered at my first encounter as Santa, I pointed to Autumn when I said be a good boy and I pointed to Oscar when I said be a good girl. Oscar immediately pointed out that Autumn would be a good GIRL and he would be a good BOY. Children can be so forgiving.

We said our goodbyes and parted with five beaming faces, Oscar, Autumn, Mom, Dad, and a brand new

Santa Claus. That was when I knew what my retirement vocation would be.

— SANTA HUGH

SANTA TRIVIA: If a house does not have a chimney, then Santa uses magic dust to make one appear and then disappear . . . Santa's toy bag is bottomless and stays full until he makes all his deliveries to children all over the world . . . Blitzen has been struck by lightning so many times, his compass always points to the North Pole . . . Prancer and Dancer are twins . . . and Rudolph always carries a back-up battery.

Christmas Photo

I'll always believe I was picked to play Santa for an indoor shopping mall because of my potbelly and my ability to grow a beard. I only lasted one year but it was jammed full of memories. This mall was downtown and attached to a very classy hotel in an NFL city.

One Friday night about twelve days before Christmas, we were packed all evening. Long lines of kids had their lists of Christmas wishes. About 8:00 P.M. at the end of the line were two of the biggest men I have ever seen.

They were huge, and they resembled each other. All of a sudden they were recognized, and kids started shouting their names, and scrambling with paper and pen for autographs. They signed them all.

If I were to mention their names, you would know immediately about whom I'm talking. Then the young man with them slid over and quietly asked me how late would we be open tomorrow night, Saturday night?

I said, "The mall closes at nine and I'll be here 'til then." He said, "See you tomorrow night." And off all three went, to the hotel where the visiting NFL team was staying.

Saturday night at the mall was almost as busy as Friday night. But it all started to clear out about 8:30. Then I began to look around to see if the two massive football players were going to show. As the old clock on the wall ticked away, it looked like they weren't going to make it.

Then, at one minute after nine, all three suddenly appeared, and the third man was holding a camera.

I smilingly said, "Ho, Ho, Ho, what do you really want for Christmas?" The answer, "A picture. With both of us sitting on your lap."

I exclaimed, "You're kidding. You'll crush me."

"Come on, Santa, we'll be very delicate."

They did sit lightly, and we laughed and posed and had an instantly great time. They were really fun to be around. In fact, I asked for a copy of the best photo of the three of us. I gave them my address and they presented me with two tickets to Sunday's sold-out NFL game.

They had to get back for bed check, but before they left, I asked what was so important about the picture with me. The oldest said, "Where we grew up there never was a Santa Claus and there never was a Christmas. My brother and I promised each other that one day, in celebration of all those Christmases we missed, we would have our picture taken sitting on Santa Claus' lap."

They did send me that picture and it's still one of my prize possessions. Every Christmas it has a special place on my mantle. It always causes a lot of conversation—you see, all three of us are black.

— SANTA (Retired)

A Christmas Wish

I'm a sergeant in the U.S. Army, and I'm stationed in North Carolina. By now, almost everybody knows that a lot of men are sent to Iraq from this part of the country; so, as hard as we try, Christmas is still not very merry.

My Commanding Officer thought we could at least pick up a little spirit for the kids by having Santa appear in the PX. He then suggested (ORDERED) my appearance in a full red uniform, with a non-regulation white beard.

So there I was with my brand new, all-white beard, (pasted on), which we borrowed from the drama department of the local college. I was surrounded by several elves, whom I outranked, along with some nurses who volunteered to be Santa's helpers.

Our first weekend was not a complete smash. In fact, if it had been one of the exhibition boxing matches in the base gym, it would have been stopped for lack of action.

But the next weekend was a different story. The word got around that we were handing out free candy, so everybody showed up. As you can imagine, most of the kids were with their mothers, because their dads were off, busy doing something else.

I had the feeling that most of the kids had been prompted by their mothers to just ask for a few presents they had written down on a piece of paper. It was all going along smoothly; even my Commanding Officer had a smile on his face when he checked on us.

Then a five-year-old boy, all dressed up in his combat khakis, with his mother at his side, climbed on my lap. He had a very serious look on his face. He wadded up his piece of paper, leaned into my ear, and whispered, "Please bring my daddy home from Iraq."

All I could think of was to whisper, "I'll do what I can." He whispered back, "That's good enough for me." And then, with a big smile on his face, he took his mother's hand and led her outside.

I really wasn't ready for his request and it stayed with me not only throughout the Christmas season but also throughout most of the next year. An Army base may look big, but it really isn't. Every once in a while I would run into that youngster and he seemed as happy as you can be under those circumstances. Then in the fall, I got real busy and forgot all about Santa Claus.

December came and my Commanding Officer reminded me what a great Santa I was, so here we go again. It was about the third weekend when I looked up and there was the young boy in his combat khakis with a big smile on his face and a firm grip on his dad's left hand.

His dad leaned forward in his well-worn combat khakis and said, "My son tells me you promised him last Christmas that you would do what you could to bring me home. I appreciate your good work." Then his son gave me a great big hug and said, "This is the best Christmas I ever had."

It wasn't until they turned away that I was aware the son was still gripping his dad's left hand because his right arm was missing. I think I'm the only one who noticed.

— SERGEANT SANTA

A POW Christmas

Christmas as a POW in 1970 during the Vietnam War was a rather non-event situation. But that year, we *virtually* "drew names from a hat" and were charged with imagining the shopping and presentation of a gift to the person's whose name we drew.

My name was drawn by Navy Lt (jg) Tim Sullivan of Boston. One of the things I had mentioned to Tim was my modest collection of beer mugs. These were not the porcelain kind available in stores, but rather ones that reflected a particular place or event.

I had collected beer mugs from the Air Force Academy and during the travels I made while a cadet, including some from an orientation tour I had taken with the Navy, one from RAF Bentwaters in England where I was stationed before going to Vietnam, and one recognizing the beer most commonly available at DaNang, a Korean brew called National.

I had expressed my frequent enjoyment of beers from around the world and often exchanged lists with others who were "beer-wise." In fact, for about a year, each night before climbing under the mosquito net, we would communicate through the walls with our tap code, the traditional GN-GBU, Good Night-God Bless You, followed by the name of a beer.

I did this with Major Don Burns, and we never repeated the name of any beer during our nightly routine. To be sure, we were enlisting the aid of others to keep the list fresh and new, and it was fun.

So when Tim Sullivan described his present, a pewter mug with engraving recognizing the year and circumstance, I greatly accepted his imaginary gift. This was all done in "make believe," but at Christmas 1973, Tim's gift did indeed arrive, at my home here in America, inscribed exactly as he had presented it while we were in Hanoi just three years before. I still have that Christmas mug along with a few other mugs that, like me, have survived.

For my part, the Christmas name I "drew" was First Lt. Garland Kramer. During a period when we were actually sharing quarters, Garland and I fashioned a deck of cards from bits of paper.

For some reason, we would always end a Black Jack session with a few hands of Old Maid. He was a world-class Black Jack and Old Maid player (I never could figure that out), and I eventually owed him 240 Baby Ruth candy bars.

So, when the time came to present gifts, I recognized his passion for Baby Ruth candy bars by presenting him with a "make believe" ornately decorated collection of boxes and boxes of his favorite candy bar. This, too, was in reality sent to him at Christmas in 1973.

This was a fun exercise for all of us and many guys did send their "pretend" gifts of 1970 after we were repatriated in 1973. I can still remember some of the presents that were described in such great detail to all of the men in that room during the *virtual* exchange.

This was the only Christmas when we had a group larger than three or four together. The Son Tay raid had occurred in November, 1970, and the North Vietnamese pulled us all in from the outlying camps into the Hoa Lo, Hanoi Hilton facility downtown, lest another attempt at rescuing POWs be mounted.

We were together for only a few months and by March 1971, the Vietnamese started spreading us out to keep us from becoming too organized for their purposes. I spent Christmas 1972 in a 7'x7' cell on the Chinese border with one other man, so Christmas 1970 was the highlight reel for the holiday season.

To be perfectly honest, I get just a bit melancholy each year at Christmas as I recall the unique camaraderie we shared in North Vietnam, and I pray for all those who were killed in action and never had the chance to be a part of the relative happiness and good fortune we POWs shared.

—SANTA ED (Maj. Gen. USAF, Retired)

My Dad— Santa Claus

I want you to go back in time with me, to Christmas Eve more than four decades ago, because not everyone has Santa Claus as their Dad.

Of course, I didn't find out until it was too late for that fact to do me any good with my grade school peers, but I can tell you it's never been short of wondrous.

Dad worked for a beverage distributor on the west side of Chicago as a warehouseman and truck driver. His generally gruff demeanor was betrayed by an engaging grin and his gentleness.

Dad had the physique for his role as Santa, with his stout, barrel chest; a ruddy, weathered nose; twinkling, steel blue eyes; and thinning hair that allowed for pin-point accuracy in placing a snowy white Santa wig on his head.

Most of all, he was always great with children. I think a lot of it is the fact that he always thought like a kid. This is clearly a family trait, this propensity for being basically immature. Dad, mother, brother, sister, and I have never let our "inner child" out—and we just wouldn't let our "adulthood" in.

I was breathless when my mom told me about Dad's secret. You can't imagine the pride I felt when I realized that the rapturous look on hundreds of kids' faces, when they're on Santa's lap, was directed at my own father.

Sometimes Dad would make house calls. People would call him to appear at Christmas parties and private family gatherings. After hauling around barrels and cases of beer throughout the city of Chicago, he would miss dinner, bolt into the bedroom, change into his red suit, wig, and beard, and bolt out again.

No matter how hurried he was, he always took time to use glue to firmly attach his mustache and apply a small amount of white shoe polish to his eyebrows. He looked just like every picture of Santa you have ever seen. (I was never sure how he got the shoe polish out of his eyebrows.)

One very cold Christmas Eve, the heater in our 1963 Chevy Bel-Air went out. Dad had to scrape the frost off the inside of the windows just to see if he could drive. He had a lot of appearances to make on this night of nights, and my brother and I wanted to go along for the first time. Naturally, Mother objected. "No, you'll freeze! The heater's broken."

"No, we won't." We countered with sweaters, sweatshirts, two pairs of pants, four pairs of socks, boots, and blankets. We promised not to be any trouble at all. Dad smiled, my mother grinned, and off we went.

We were cold, very cold, but we didn't freeze. Plus Mom made us a thermos of hot chocolate and lots of Christmas cookies. My brother and I got Dad to leave the keys in the car, in between stops, so we could listen to the radio while he was being Santa. Back then, WGN

Radio in Chicago had an announcer by the name of John Mallo, who spoke in a wonderful baritone.

He played Christmas songs, read Christmas poetry, and told Christmas stories, including Dylan Thomas' "Christmas in Wales" and O. Henry's "Gift of the Magi." He also gave updates from NORAD, tracking Santa's sleigh from the North Pole to Chicago. He just plain talked to us.

My brother and I would sing along with the carols and listen to the poems and stories. We drew pictures on the frost-covered car windows with our fingers until they got numb from the cold. We looked up through the back window at the sky on this night that was too cold even for clouds, and we watched for shooting stars.

When Dad made his way back to the car, we asked him about the people he met, what the kids were like and, of course, what kind of toys they got.

Dad listened patiently and answered every question we could think up. He teased us about our own Christmas list and worried about us getting cold. In fact, his caring made us a lot warmer.

It was remarkable to experience. Little by little, Santa took over Dad's personality, more and more, after each stop. It was as if we were actually riding with Santa. We all shared the hot chocolate and cookies and then my brother fell asleep on the backseat of the sleigh.

When we got home, Dad carried my brother into the house and put him to bed. On the wings of a magical night with Santa in his sleigh, with songs and poems and stories of Christmas in my head, I floated into bed.

I really don't remember what toys I got for Christmas that year, but I do know the gift my heart received: My Dad, Santa Claus.

— DEAN CURTIS
JEFF CURTIS

SANTA BULLETIN: Santa Claus is listed as #1 on *Forbes* List of the Fictional 15. Santa beat out, among others: Daddy Warbucks (#2), Lex Luthor (#4), Jed Clampett (#7), Bruce Wayne (#8), Willie Wonka (#10), and Lara Croft (#13).

"Merry Christmas, Santa"

It all began as a busy season for Santa. I had visited several homes, some department stores, plus a few pancake breakfasts, and it was only the second week of the Christmas season. Yet, when Mrs. Claus asked me to go to a local nursing home to visit a friend, I couldn't say no. Santa is not just for children, but for children of all ages.

At the nursing home, I was greeted with smile after smile. I found they all loved Santa Claus and moreover, they all loved to guess who Santa really was. In those days, I wore an artificial beard not at all like the real whiskers I sport today.

One woman in a wheelchair suggested I was one of the orderlies under my beard and another, sitting by the wall, said I was the janitor. I was thrilled just to watch their happy reactions.

Mrs. Claus and I went to our friend's room where we chatted for several minutes. She then took us visiting. I'm happy to say, the patients were all glad to see Santa. It's wonderful how we all hold a love for Santa that started in our youth, and we never let that inner child grow old.

After visiting many of the rooms, we said goodbye and were turning to leave when a nurse came up and asked, "Santa, would you mind visiting a friend of mine?" I said we would be glad to and as we walked down the corridor, she told us this man had suffered a severe stroke about six months ago and had not spoken a word since. His wife, who sat with him daily, was heartbroken and a visit from Santa Claus might do them good.

Upon entering the room, the nurse went over to the man's wife and told her she had brought a friend to see them. The man in the bed had his head turned away from us, facing the only window in the room.

I stepped up to the bed, placed my gloved hand into his, and said softly, "Merry Christmas." I looked at his wife who was smiling. Suddenly, the man turned his face toward me and looked me over. Then, laboring to smile, he opened his mouth and slowly said, "Merry Christmas, Santa."

After six months of not speaking to anyone, he directed his first words to Santa Claus. There was not a dry eye in the room. I looked down and told him that he had been a good boy and I was proud of him, and that Mrs. Claus and Santa would be praying for him. He smiled bigger than Christmas. After hugging his wife, we left.

Santa had a purpose that day, to give love to someone who really needed the Spirit of Christmas. I am still happy that *this* Santa Claus was chosen for the job. The magic of Santa is true and can be shared by all.

— SANTA JOHN AND MRS. CLAUS

"Santa 'Spoke' to Me

Just this past Christmas, Santa and I were at a "Come See" Santa and Mrs. Claus photo opportunity, at a local gift store. Many people came, including one family with a boy and two girls.

While the boy and one of the girls rushed up to talk with Santa, the other girl, about eight years old, held back. She had no expression on her face and didn't speak to anyone.

They all sat on our laps for photos and then started to leave. That's when the photographer whispered in my ear that the real quiet girl was deaf. I told Santa, and he asked someone to please get her attention.

When she turned around, he signed, "God bless you." Oh my, I will never forget that darling child's face as she totally lit up, jumping up and down, and signing, "Santa 'spoke' to me! Santa 'spoke' to me! Santa 'spoke' to me!"

— MRS. NINA CLAUS

Santa Discovered

I'm a large guy, weighing in at 317 pounds. (I wasn't kidding.) I have salt-and-pepper hair and a handlebar mustache I keep all year. I usually wear red as it gets close to Christmas with the word "Santa" embroidered on all items.

During the rest of the year, when I'm on my way home, I wear shirts with the colors and name of the college where I work as the gardening supervisor.

I was in a grocery store's frozen food aisle one evening, looking for something to take home for dinner. As I walked up and down each aisle trying to decide, I noticed a little girl with her father looking at me. I smiled at her and went on with my search. However, I noticed that the little girl kept watching me and watching me and watching me.

Now, here's the scene. It was not even close to Christmas. I did not have any red clothing on. My hair and mustache were their natural colors, and I had no beard.

The little girl finally went to her father and tugged at his coat sleeve. After she did this a couple of times, her father leaned down and asked what she wanted.

She pointed at me and said loud enough that I could hear, "Santa."

I have never gotten over that little girl picking me out as Santa. The way I was dressed and looked, how did she know I was Santa Claus?

There is a Santa saying, "It's not in the red suit and it's not in the white beard, it's in the heart." I think that little girl understood.

— SANTA LOWELL

SANTA BULLETIN: When you visit Santa's Village, be sure to check your "Naughty and Nice Rating."™ It's never too late to find out how you stand with Santa.

No More Milk
and Cookies

One Christmas Eve my elf and I had nearly completed our regular route. We had been delivering gifts to some little ones who otherwise might not get anything for Christmas, let alone special gifts from Santa in person. Our traditional last stop is a friend's house where we usually share a meal before heading home.

That evening when I called to let them know we were on our way, my friend asked us for a favor. He was going to call his favorite Mexican restaurant and wanted to know if we could stop by and pick up meals for everyone. I replied, "No problem."

We were still in full costume when we got to the restaurant. We figured we would slip in as quietly as possible, through the front door, then around the counter to the kitchen, so as not to make a scene. "T'was a bad idea."

We had not been there for more than two minutes before a little head peeped around the corner. We could hear in the background, "It's him!" "It can't be!" "What would he be doing here?" Every couple of minutes a new head would appear and then quickly disappear.

Let's face it, we couldn't disappoint them. So as soon as our order arrived and our bill was paid, my elf and Santa Claus entered the main dining room. There were gasps and giggles and cheers galore as we slowly worked our way around the room.

I explained to them that we had a long night ahead and needed some good food to get us underway. I also reminded the youngsters to go to bed on time tonight and close their eyes extra tight because I couldn't go down a chimney if there were any children awake in the house.

That was when it happened. One little girl promised very sincerely that she would be in bed on time and that she would leave me milk and cookies. I couldn't help but notice the extra large bowl on the table, which had formerly held guacamole, so I quipped, "Milk and cookies are nice, but what I'd REALLY like is guacamole and chips." My elf then signaled it was time for us to go, so I did my final, "Ho, Ho, Ho," and we headed for the door.

A couple of weeks later, back in our civvies, we stopped by that Mexican restaurant for lunch. A few minutes after we ordered, the manager came by our table. He wanted to thank us for our Christmas Eve performance and to tell us that every child in the restaurant went home with at least one takeout order of guacamole and chips!

— SANTA DAVE

Santa's Policeman

"T'was the week before Christmas" . . . and this real bearded Santa was southbound on his way to visit children at a private party. The highway narrowed from four lanes to two as I proceeded through the intersection. Half a block later, the car in front of me stopped, waiting for traffic to clear before turning left into a fast food drive-in. I stopped, too, and then there was this crunching sound.

Two thoughts immediately went through my mind. The first was, Santa is going to be late. The second was, At least I won't have to wait long for a policeman, because all I could see in my rear-view mirror was the light bar on the police cruiser that had just rear-ended *me.*

The sound of the crash, of course, attracted the attention of diners in the drive-in, people in their cars, and others on the sidewalk in front of the nearby shops.

As the policeman got out of his car, this audience was aware that he was at fault. They were very quiet and watching closely to see how he would handle the situation. I can imagine he was already quite embarrassed, but he had to be totally crestfallen when I stepped out of my car—full beard, black boots, red suit, white trim, and a Santa stocking cap.

The crowd went wild.

A week before Christmas, and the cop hit Santa!

I assured him that I was physically okay, but the front license plate bracket on his patrol car had punctured two holes on the bumper of my brand new (four-month-old) Honda Civic.

The officer said I had two choices: I could file a claim against the county (which would put his career in jeopardy and cause a whole lot of headaches) or he would take care of the damage. We agreed that my car would be fixed and that he would pay for the repairs.

Everyone applauded when we drove away.

I took the car to a local dealer who employs a "ding" repair specialist. He wet-sanded the damaged areas, patched and filled the holes, sanded and primed the repair, and repainted the whole bumper. It was a beautiful job.

As I described it to the policeman, I could feel the cash register "ka-chinging" in his head—dealer, sanded, patched, primer, two coats of paint, entire bumper. He asked for the final total, and I told him, "Fifty dollars." He was stunned. He was expecting considerably more. That's when I told him he needed to hear the rest of the story.

This Santa's "Mrs. Claus" is a piano teacher during the rest of the year. She taught two very talented sisters who faced a crisis several years ago.

Their father had been injured and was out of work for several months. Their mother had to go back to work and the children had to be pulled out of most of their outside activities because of the loss of income. Piano was one of those extras.

My bride and I decided that these two young ladies had actually earned "scholarships" that allowed them to continue their lessons for the next three months.

Piano became the one area of stability in a summer that was very turbulent, and they were most appreciative. That's right, their dad was the "ding" repair specialist. I never saw an itemized bill, but I'm convinced he only charged me for materials, if even that.

I told the policeman I was not hurt, I did not want to sue, my car was damaged, but the total cost for repairs was $50.00—and it was a first-class job.

The police officer was silent for a few moments. He then said, "I'm not used to dealing with people like you. Maybe I really *did* bump into Santa Claus after all!"

— SANTA CHARLIE

SANTA BULLETIN: True story. The policeman is still on active duty. Santa does not wish to name him or his rank, or identify his department. After all, it *is* Christmas.

Santa in the Nation's Capitol

One of the most exciting and sought after gigs for Santa is to be a part of the Pageant of Peace and the lighting of the National Christmas Tree. All of this takes place in early December on the Ellipse just opposite the White House in Washington, D.C. The program traditionally features joyous holiday music from an outstanding children's choir, plus a host of other talented performers.

So, you can understand that I was both delighted and honored to be asked to play Santa at the Pageant of Peace and excited about having the opportunity to be my very best Santa. I knew that I had several things going for me.

I am big enough not to need to stuff a pillow into the front of my suit, and I also have a beard and mustache that are getting whiter every year, which helps to give me a natural North Pole look.

I have to confess that I was very anxious as I waited nervously to make my big entry with sleigh bells ringing and lots of little children eyeing me cautiously. However, my appearance with plenty of booming, "HO, HO, HOs," went smoothly. Then I sat down and read "The Night Before Christmas," accompanied by the Coast Guard Band.

The highlight of the evening was having the president there for the lighting of the beautiful National Tree and knowing that I would have the opportunity to meet both President and Mrs. Bush as they made their way onstage at the conclusion of the festivities.

The president came down the line of performers, shaking hands and visiting, when he finally got to me, he looked me in the eye, smiled, and said, "Well, it was nice to have a Santa who could keep his pants up."

It turns out the previous Santa lost his red trousers as he climbed up on the stage, which left a distinct impression on the president as well as on the crowd.

I have been fortunate enough to be invited back to the Pageant of Peace to once again put on my bright red suit. Believe me, I always make sure that I have a belt, suspenders, and even a roll of silver duct tape, just to be sure. I certainly don't want a headline that reads, "Santa Makes Best Showing of Evening."

— SANTA MERLIN #74

"Santa's Book"

Santa Claus knows he can't really promise anything to the children who visit him. After all, he needs to check his inventory at the North Pole, and confer with his elves to see if they have certain items; and, of course, he has to check his 'Naughty and Nice' book.

As I have grown in my role as Santa, I have decided that there really isn't a 'Naughty and Nice' book. I believe in my heart that, to Santa, all children who believe in him belong on the 'Nice' list.

For that reason, I carry a little red book with me in which I write down the names of the children who visit me and a word or two about their Christmas wishes.

Over the years, the names in my "Santa's Book" have grown and grown. I can even go through the pages and remind my regular visitors about their requests in previous years. It really surprises them when I ask if they enjoyed the Barbie Doll or the fire truck I left them last year.

Also, as my book has become filled, I can usually find any name that I am looking for, so it has become a valuable "ice breaker." Often, children want to know if their name is in "Santa's Book," so, together, we look for it. Their eyes light up as they intently search the pages looking for their own name.

If after a few pages we don't find it, I just tell them I will have to write it in. Then, with pen in hand, they tell me their name, then spell it, and what they want for Christmas. I can see and feel the sense of security that it gives the children knowing that their name is in "Santa's Book."

During one special visit, a young lad about seven years old, hung to the back of the line, until he was sure he would have a private audience with Santa. After he climbed on my lap, we exchanged the usual greetings and then I asked him what he wanted for Christmas.

He surprised me when he told he didn't want anything for Christmas. Then he pulled me to him and whispered, "All I want for Christmas is for the rest of the children in my school to quit picking on me and calling me names."

My heart just broke, as I had felt the exact same way when I was his age. It broke again when I realized he believed that Santa could fix it. I knew there was no way I could make a difference. That was a promise that Santa simply could not make.

All of a sudden I remembered that I had my "Santa's Book" inside my suit coat. As I took it out, I said to the young man, "I understand how you feel, son, but Santa can't be with you all the time when other children are picking on you. I'm afraid that Santa can't make them stop. But here's what I can do. I'm going to write your name in "Santa's Book" and when I get home tonight, I promise that I will say my prayers for you." The biggest, warmest smile came over that young lad's face as he replied, "Okay." That was all he needed to hear. I gave him a big hug and he was on his way.

Just as he climbed down off my lap, I felt as though the Holy Spirit was speaking to me, "That is a promise that you can keep, Santa!" So that night in bed, I took out my "Santa's Book," turned to the page with the young man's name, and began to talk to God about his request.

All of a sudden I felt as if heaven opened up. As I talked, it was as if every angel was listening to my request. I knew in my heart that my prayers for this boy were being heard.

I have entered many names and circumstances into what I now call "Santa's Prayer Book." As I search the pages for their names, the book still delights children of all ages. Many remember the book and ask me to bring it out. I even had a special pocket sewn in my red coat to carry it.

The greatest significance of the book is that it represents the privilege I have to keep Santa's promise to pray for the names and requests hidden in its pages. I now realize that when I pray for these children, I may be the only person who has ever lifted their name to heaven.

What an awesome privilege I have to represent such precious children and their dreams! And what confidence I now have that there is one promise that Santa can *always* keep!

— SANTA CLIFF

The Magic of Santa

I was visiting with children at our local Kmart store when I first met them. They were standing across the aisle from where Santa's display was located. It was a grandmother with her granddaughter, who was ten years old. At first glance, they didn't have much in the way of material things; they were dressed in over-washed hand-me-downs.

I could tell the little girl really wanted to speak with me, so I finished with the small boy on my lap and then motioned her up. She perched on my left knee and smiled as the interview began. I immediately knew this was going to be something special.

All she wanted was a copy of a new Christmas video that had just been released and a new pair of warm pants. However, when she told me this, her grandmother stepped forward and immediately said, in a careworn voice, "Honey, Santa is going to have a hard time at our house this year."

I asked what she meant and she explained that they were living in a small trailer on a very fixed income with three other children, all younger than the one on my knee.

The local aid programs had not fulfilled their promise and with Christmas just five days away, they had no money or means to provide Christmas. At this, the little girl just seemed to shrink.

I immediately gave her a hug and told her, "Christmas is a time of great love and miracles. Don't give up, and don't stop believing. There will be a way." With this, she smiled and joined her grandmother. "I hope you're right," the older woman said as they turned and walked away.

As I watched them go back down the aisle, something within me began to churn and a determined voice within my heart began to speak. It said, "Okay, Santa, are you going to sit here or are you going to give this family the best Christmas they could ever have?"

There was no one in line to see me so I put up my "Santa has to feed his reindeer" sign and went in search of a store manager. When I found one, I asked her if Kmart would be willing to help me perform some Christmas magic? I was told, they sure would.

I explained the situation and then I asked her to be on the lookout for the grandmother and granddaughter because I needed to talk with them before they left the store.

When they returned to the Santa display, the grandmother asked me, "What is it, Santa?" I said, "Santa is going to make a Special Delivery Christmas." She then smiled as I wrote down names, their address and phone number, and everyone's sizes. I told her I would call the next day. There were hugs all around, and tears in our eyes.

When I explained what had happened to my wife, Michelle, she said, "How do you plan to do this?" As always, Mrs. Claus was keeping my feet on the ground. I explained to her that God would take care of it. And indeed He did. That night at church I was asked about my Special Delivery Christmas by friends who immediately gave us money.

My prayers, however, were just beginning to be answered. With our own money and that which was donated, we bought toys, books, and decorations for the family and prepared to take them over the next day. I called, just as I said I would, and set a time. All was going well and it appeared that Christmas had been saved.

However, when Mrs. Claus and I got to the address, our hearts sank. As we looked over the hill, we saw the tumbled-down trailer in which the family lived. There was debris all over the yard and as I stepped onto the front porch, I nearly fell through a large hole.

As I knocked on the door, I noticed there wasn't even a doorknob. Invited inside, I found the grandmother sitting in a very shabby living room, which contained two chairs, a television, a VCR, and a table. She was wearing three shirts and a coat. There was no heat. I thought, Thank goodness, the children aren't here.

Mrs. Claus talked with the grandmother as I made my way back to the car and brought in what we had gathered so far. She cried and thanked us profusely. We then spent a few moments discussing their other needs such as heat and food. I promised to return on Christmas Eve and as we got back in the car, I said a silent prayer, "Lord, help me to help these poor people."

Once again I was heard. Mrs. Claus and I began to buy blankets and warm clothing for the four kids. I called on some friends for assistance. After all, Santa does have his helpers. I went to my best friend Karl, and he donated money for food. My family bought food and warm clothing. Friends at work pitched in with food and other needed products.

From everyone who heard what we were doing, we had donations of food, clothing, toys, and money. A woman from our church donated a Christmas tree. Kmart came through with two hundred dollars worth of gift certificates.

And finally, we bought the Christmas video the little girl had asked for that started it all. Mrs. Claus and I were absolutely amazed. By six o'clock on Christmas Eve, we had two truck loads of "Christmas" for this family.

Dressed in my red Santa suit, I gave Mrs. Claus a kiss and a wave, and calling to the reindeer, I was off with my two helpers. When I arrived at the trailer with my sister and her husband, not a creature was stirring. I issued forth some large "HO, HO, HOs," to announce my coming with my sack full of toys.

I sidestepped the hole in the porch and pushed open the door. The children immediately huddled around me with cries of "Santa! Santa!" The grandmother, with tears streaming down her face, gave me a big hug and kept saying, "I knew you would come! I knew you would come!"

As my helpers filled their house with box after box of surprises, I opened my big sack full of toys and began handing them out to the children. Their big smiles and happy faces glowed with the wonder of Christmas. We set up and decorated the tree, then put some colorful boxes under it to be opened on Christmas morning.

Now it was time to reach deep down into my bag for the present that started this whole joyous evening—the Christmas video for the little girl who lives here with her family. As she saw the top of the box she started jumping up and down and screaming, "Thank you, Santa, thank you!"

When the last toy was finally distributed, I laid my finger beside my nose and with a nod, exclaimed that I had to go. The grandmother gave me one more hug and thanked me. I told her, "This is what happens when you believe. Merry Christmas."

She said, "I always knew there was a Santa Claus and now I've met him." I quietly gave her a card with some phone numbers for additional help. Then, to the sleigh I went and gave the team a whistle and was off for some other visits I'd promised.

This entire experience taught me a wonderful lesson about Christmas. It showed me how great the Spirit of Christmas truly is and no matter how big the need or challenge, God will supply.

Considering all of the love created by so many people in this act of giving, and the smiles and tears of sheer joy, I can only conclude that the magic of Santa truly is real.

— SANTA JOHN

I Believe

I had an appointment at the salon for a touch-up on my beard. I walked in wearing my red Santa hat and my glasses. The stylists said it would be a few minutes so I sat down. It was really warm that day and the lady who owns the salon asked the stylist to open the door to let in some fresh air.

At that very moment, a small gust of wind blew the door open. The timing could not have been more perfect. The owner looked over at me and I winked. She said, rather loudly, "Oh my God, you *are* real!" I answered, "That's right. And remember, I know if you have been naughty or nice." The lady whose nails she was doing replied, "I'm in big trouble."

Even adults without a single kid around still want to believe.

— SANTA MICHAEL

SANTA BULLETIN: Santa is real to those who believe he is real.

Christmas

One of the great things about being Santa Claus at Christmas is that you get to witness the best in all people. I will always remember this youngster who just wanted to sit on Santa's lap. But his mother said no, because she thought you had to pay to see Santa.

You could tell she was financially strapped and when the youngster was then allowed to sit on my lap, he pleaded for his picture with Santa. Before I could do anything, the lady next in line quietly told the photographer to take the picture and she would pay for it.

Wouldn't it be wonderful if it was Christmas all year 'round?

— **SANTA CLAUS**
(Martin Lebowitz's
legal middle name)

SANTA'S POEM:

The night was perfect for our sleigh,
The stars were bright to guide our way,
Rudolph's nose was a brilliant red,
So we followed him, just as he said.

"Other Voices – Other Sleighs"

First Boy: "Santa doesn't hold a full-time job!"

Second Boy: "Yes, he does. How do you think he pays for all those toys at Christmas?"

"Whenever my grandson Travis sees a picture of Santa, he always points and says, 'There's Papa!' "

"I heard a noise on Christmas Eve, so I got out of my bed and went halfway down the stairs. Then I saw you. I was so frightened I ran upstairs, jumped into my bed and pulled the covers over my head. I've waited thirty years to tell you that."

"The reason I want the children asleep is so I can deliver their presents and then quickly move on to the house next door. If all the children were awake on Christmas Eve, I would want to visit with them and I wouldn't have time to deliver all the toys and gifts."

"In Germany, a few days before St. Nicholas Day, the children dress up in costumes like on Halloween. They go from store to store to collect candy. They come in groups and sing special songs in the dialect of the region in which they live. This is a very colorful event in the cities."

"My wife made my first Santa suit and at the same time she made a Mrs. Claus dress for herself. Because we did not want our youngest daughter to know what was happening, the suit and the dress were made during the night when she was sleeping."

"After asking the kids what they all wanted for Christmas, I took a moment to share what I hoped the elves were bringing me for Christmas—-some hair as I was getting bald. Then I took off my red stocking cap to show them I wasn't kidding."

"His wife said he'd been a loner kind of guy. But, since he had his heart valve repaired, he was a completely different person, sharing the wonders of of the season with his entire family. We saw the true spirit of Christmas come to life in an adult."

"Sometimes a child will reach out and touch your heart. I'll always remember the little girl who only wanted a colored pencil for Christmas, so that she could color in her coloring book."

"Even at Christmas a 'Bad Apple' can work its way into our barrel. I did hear about a 'Bad Santa' down in Florida. It seems he lost his cool with a youngster who was a fan of the 'wrong' college football team. That's a real, 'Bah, Humbug.' "

"I'll always remember the Christmas I became aware that the Santa I had believed in all those years was not a physical being who came down the chimney or through the door on Christmas Eve. Instead he was represented in love through my Mom and Dad."

"I once had a daughter bring her eighty-six-year-old mother for a picture with Santa. She told me she was returning the favor for all the times when she was a young girl and her mother had taken her for a picture with Santa. Her mother was just beaming."

"My 'Santa's Brother' has his own mission. On Christmas Eve he and his wife open their home to members of the local alcohol and drug abuse recovery chapters for a dinner for anyone who doesn't have a family with whom to share Christmas. He is living proof that God has a wonderful plan for all our lives."

"The True Spirit of Christmas Lies in Your Heart."

A Special Hour

A couple of years ago I was appearing at a charity party for the San Onofre Marine Families. This group caters to Marine families who have had one of their parents deployed away from them at Camp Pendleton, California.

A young girl of about four was completely enamored with my "goings on." While she was a darling, much to the chagrin of many of the families, she never left my side and was often attached to my leg. In spite of her mom's best efforts, she probably appeared in more pictures with Santa than all the other families combined.

Then in two weeks, I was in the midst of Christmas Eve and one of my best friends asked if I could drop by her house because she was entertaining a special family. Just as I finished placing some gifts under her tree, I started toward the door, and that same little girl came around the corner with her mom, carrying a bag of trash.

We spent a lovely hour together and she had Santa basically all to herself on Christmas Eve. I'm certain she is going to believe in Santa Claus well into her adult years!

—SANTA JOE

A Gothic Christmas

In my first year as Santa, as I was ready to "feed the reindeer" and leave for the night, a teenage boy dressed in "Gothic" approached me and asked for my autograph. I told him I was on my way out, but I would be back the next morning.

He was there first thing in the morning and I signed a small, torn, scrap of paper – "Santa Claus." Later that day, the boy was back with three friends, all in black, with multicolored, spiked hair, and multiple piercings.

The four stood in line behind toddlers and families for about twenty-five minutes to see me. When their turn came, they approached my chair and stood in a semicircle in front of me. We chatted about how they were doing and what was on their minds. After about five minutes, as they prepared to go, one asked, "Santa, can we have a hug?" I got up and gave each of them a BIG HUG and a big "Merry Christmas."

I learned that memorable Christmas presents sometimes come in strangely wrapped packages.

—SANTA JERRY

Santa's Helper

A couple of years ago I was in the local Wal*Mart with my teenage son, looking at toys. This was before I would bleach my hair and beard for Christmas, so my hair was black and my full beard was reddish brown. I had on my red Santa hat that I wear from Thanksgiving on, denim bib overalls, a flannel shirt, and black mud boots.

I overheard this little boy tell his mom, "There's one of Santa's helpers." She told him, no it wasn't. He said it was. So I turned to him and asked, "Have you been a good boy?" He said he had. I then said, "Do you always keep your room neat and clean?" His mother had to muffle a laugh. He mumbled, "Sometimes." I then told him to be good because Christmas is close and I'll be watching for Santa.

We then left for another department and while standing there, I felt a tug on my shirt. Turning, I saw the little boy again. He said, "I'm on my way home with mom and as soon as we get there, I'm going to clean my room."

—SANTA MICHAEL

Matchmaker

Weddings are always memorable, but what about the proposal? A young man once asked if he could propose to his fiancé while sitting on my lap. I told him I would be honored. They were going to come by on Saturday and I was just to ask him what he wanted for Christmas.

When the staff saw him in line, they came to tell me he would be up shortly. Then, as he and his fiancé sat on my lap, I asked my usual question, "And what would you like for Christmas?"

This young man then made the most beautiful statement. He told about the years when he wanted material things. But, as he grew older, he realized there were more important things in life. He said he wanted his fiancé to be a part of his life forever.

He then bent on one knee and asked her, "Will you marry me?" This was a moving experience for everyone. The girl's jaw dropped; she was truly surprised. She started shaking, but not before she gave a beautiful, "Yes." Then they kissed.

As I looked around, we were all wiping our eyes.

—SANTA CLAUS LEBOWITZ

The Horse-Drawn Sleigh

I was sitting in a beautiful sleigh, waiting my turn in the Christmas Parade. The sleigh was being pulled by a big, handsome, black Percheron horse. The owner of the horse had asked if her six-year-old little girl, who was wearing a cute red and white Santa hat, could ride in the sleigh with me. Of course, I said, "Yes!"

She asked me questions about the reindeer, flying the sleigh at night, and sliding down chimneys. I tried to answer all her questions. Then, I commented on the beauty of the horse pulling the sleigh. She replied that he was her horse. She continued, "I feed him, give him his water, and even brush him every day. Mommy says I should take good care of him 'cause he's the one who jumps on the back of the other horses and makes the little ones."

I did all I could to keep from bursting out laughing. Then I looked down at her mom, who had overheard the conversation. She had turned and was quickly walking away, shaking with laughter.

—SANTA BUD

The Month Before Christmas

T'was the month before Christmas, when into the mall,
came Jerry, the teacher, to follow his call.

His beard and his hair were nearly all white,
with suit of red felt, his fit was just right.

The children would come to sit on his knees,
and beg for gifts, 'neath fake Christmas trees.

He'd sit and he'd listen, ten hours at a stretch,
his lunch and his dinner, others would fetch.

A babe three days old he was given to hold,
a gift to this man, more precious than gold.

A grandma of ninety-seven, on his knee did she sit,
"I've been a good girl," she was quick to admit.

With children in tow, the grandmas did come,
Santa's knees were still ready, but sometimes felt numb.

A student from my past, to Santa did bring,
her siblings, herself, and her brand new offspring.

Teachers who knew him, from a distance would wave,
"Ho, ho!" he'd shout. "Be sure to behave."

When children were few, Santa's gaze it would wander,
watching mothers and fathers, with money to squander.

A red-haired trio, to Santa did tell,
their wishes and hopes, for this coming Noel.

The lines would get long, his throat would get sore,
from talking too much, this man most adore.

Tall players from Utah around him did lean,
these women a dozen, a basketball team.

Some toddlers with ties, and with dresses they'd wear,
for photos just perfect, with grandpas to share.

"What books might you like?" he'd ask a young child,
who just wanted some noise to drive mama wild.

Famous Barbie and Ken were wanted by many,
he'd listen and nod, and wished there weren't any.

Families would sit, and for pictures they'd pay,
this man wearing red, seeing flashes all day.

Esther, Tim, Clare, and Austin, to visit they came,
these sons and these daughters, who honor his name.

Santa's honey, too, put her arms 'round his neck,
this woman named Pat, he gave her a peck.

A toddler named Taylor was puzzled and said,
"I saw Santa at the library, also in red."

The days moved on, toward Christmas Eve,
he helped many little ones, still wanting to believe.

This tale is near done but Santa, don't fear,
will be back in this spot, near the end of next year.

He loves this new role, with joy he can share,
with all who will visit with him in his chair.

—SANTA JERRY

Santa's Audition

I went on an audition as Santa Claus for a commercial. A mother was there with her eight-year-old son and six-year-old daughter. The little girl said, "You're not Santa Claus." Her brother immediately said, "Oh, I think he is." The little girl replied, "If you are really Santa Claus, then do some magic."

I told her I was not going to prove who I really was. Instead, I pulled out my Sleigh License with my official Santa photo and gave it to her brother. He looked at it and read, "Claus, Santa, One Snowflake Lane, North Pole." Then he added, "It's him alright!" We were then called in to audition.

After it was over, we left together. An elevator came with only room enough for their family, so I remained on the nineteenth floor. Immediately after, an empty elevator arrived and I expressed to the lobby. After a quick exit, I stood in front of their elevator with my arms folded. When the door opened, the little girl eyes got real big and she screamed, "How did you get here?"

I slowly unfolded my arms and said, "MAGIC."

Her brother laughed, "I told you so!"

I quickly left, thinking, "We have another believer."

—SANTA TOM

Ho, Ho, Ho!

I'll never forget the first and only time I ever had a chance to be Santa Claus. I can remember, like it was yesterday. I was in the sixth grade in public school.

When the parts for the annual Christmas Pageant were being given out, I was selected as Santa Claus. To say that was the happiest time of my life, would even today be an understatement. With actors sprinkled throughout my family, I just knew this was my big break. This year, Santa Claus—next year, Broadway.

However, I did stumble onto one problem. I was having a difficult time capturing the jolly "ho, ho, hos" that set Santa apart from all of the non-speaking, colorful giant boxes under the tree in the middle of the stage.

As I continued my struggle during the rehearsals, one of the other boys—you know the kind: He started shaving in the sixth grade—shouted from his box, "Like this Santa, 'HO, HO, HO.'" All of the teachers immediately turned around. I knew I was dead in the water.

We switched parts. I was now a non-speaking, Jack-in-the-Box. Perhaps, that's when I first thought about a career in medicine.

—DOCTOR SANTA

santa cool

Got a little tale to tell . . . the cool part is playing the sax . . . yes, that's right . . . when santa was on his way to a gig . . . but had another appointment just before, at the shrink's office . . . believe it, even santa has problems that can occasionally overwhelm and need a little extra smooth guidance . . . you know, to get through it . . . i had then been diagnosed with a nasty terminal something . . . really wasn't coping well . . . after a couple of months, it all came together . . . well, on this particular day . . . snow was sticking . . .

my doctor john, ha, that's his real name . . . his office was shared by a couple of other mind/head specialist types who dealt with children of different ages . . . that same young fellow, about ten, usually waiting in the waiting room . . . same time as me . . . his reaction to seeing me was priceless . . . i was in full santa gear . . . red suit, fake beard, big bag, colored boxes . . . i entered the office, and there he was sitting with his mother . . . he looked at me . . . i nodded, looked at him . . . he looked at his mother . . . i looked at his mother . . . she said, see, even santa has problems . . . the kid was agitated . . . he says a little louder . . . i thought i had problems, but now you're telling me santa does, too, and worse . . . there was a long, quiet moment . . . i didn't know how to respond . . . then their doctor entered and the three of them left the waiting room . . .

i continued to my appointment as santa instead of me . . . my doctor took it all in kind, and i related what occurred in the waiting room . . . seems the lad had some heavy emotional problems based on trusting people . . . my doctor mentioned the incident might have been a negative or a positive . . . now that's really going out on a mistletoe limb . . . i said, regardless, his mother will be talking about it for years . . . and that's one of the things i enjoy about these moments we get doing this gig . . . i try to live the life, despite the obstacles that are placed in my way . . . the spirit lives in me, and i try to keep the twinkle alive . . . glad to share . . .

> — santa warren a.k.a. santa cool.
> Canada.

santa's dictionary . . . mis-tle-toe . . . a parasite evergreen plant . . . thick leaves . . . yellowish flowers . . . good to kiss under . . . cool . . . don't eat . . . shiny, white, poisonous berries . . .

The Impersonator

This past Christmas season Papa (Santa) and I (Mrs. Claus) were beginning to feel like we missed a memo from the head office! It all began on a beautiful California winter evening, at the height of our Christmas season.

Papa and I were on our way to visit some very nice parents who had invited the rest of their family to join them in their home for a visit from Santa. However, just before we got there, we received a call on Papa's sleigh phone from our host, asking if we could briefly delay our arrival.

He explained that the local fire department had decided to put Christmas decorations on some of its fire equipment and was holding an impromptu parade, complete with Santa atop the hook and ladder.

He said his wife had just discovered on the Internet that the parade route would pass right in front of their home, at the exact time of our scheduled arrival! Since we were already in their neighborhood, Papa found an out-of-the-way place to park the sleigh and we settled in to await the all-clear sign.

After only a few minutes, the front door of the home in front of which we were parked opened wide, spilling a bright light across their front lawn. Then a man came out. Although it was dark, there was enough light from the street lamps, as well as from his own front door, that he had to know who we were. He looked curiously at us and then peered up the street.

He turned quickly and went back into his house.

Our first thought was that he was going to call the police. Instead, he and his wife both came out and stared at us. Then the wife turned and peered up the street.

By this time, I had the window down and Papa shouted, "Please don't call the police. We're just hiding until some children are ready for us." The man replied, "We weren't going to call the police; we were going to call the fire department. We thought you were their Santa, and we were wondering why you were meeting them here."

We all had a good laugh and were still chatting a few minutes later when the brightly-lit Christmas parade turned the corner at the end of their street and headed directly toward us with sirens and speakers blaring!

In a flash, all the neighborhood families were in their front yards, children cheering wildly for the obviously fake-bearded Santa on top of the fire engine! As the parade passed our car, Papa and I put the visors down in the sleigh and slid down in our seats as far as we could, our newly befriended homeowners laughing hysterically the whole time.

Before the parade had even finished passing where we were parked, the sleigh phone rang. It was our host for the evening, telling us that all their neighbors had finished wishing one another a "Merry Christmas," and gone back inside. Now would be a good time for Santa to arrive.

We bid our newfound friends goodbye and went on with our evening, with the incident quickly receding from our minds as our Christmas season heated up.

However, Papa and I couldn't resist sharing the story with the Mayor of the city as we were riding with him and his family in the cab of a city fire engine, while on our way to the official lighting of the city Christmas tree!

You see, Papa is the Official Santa for the city, and the Mayor's darling young daughter was so taken with Papa that His Honor told us afterward she had refused to eat her chicken at dinner that evening, insisting instead that it be boxed up for Santa, his reindeers, and his elves.

It should be noted that in addition to the giant Christmas tree, our city had also converted one of its most popular tourist attractions, a downtown square, into a beautiful North Pole setting.

Papa loved it. Santa's throne was out near the edge of the square so he could be clearly seen. The horn blowing and waving auto traffic came in all directions. To provide holiday music, the city also hired a series of bands for each evening.

One night, a Korean family was arranging themselves around us for a special photo, when a strange thing happened.

Suddenly, I noticed that a lot of the folks around the square were looking up the street. Car horns were blaring as usual, and then I heard a siren. I looked up, but whatever it was, was still around the corner out of my sight.

More folks on the square were moving out toward the curb, and I heard a second and then a third siren. The crowd at the curb started cheering, and I noticed many of them looking over their shoulders, back at us. Some of them were even pointing and laughing.

Next, we saw two motorcycle cops riding slowly past the square, waving, with lights flashing and sirens blaring. Following them was a police squad car, then the fire chief, a rescue truck, another squad car, and then came the city's hook-and-ladder fire truck—AND sitting right on top, waving with one hand and holding his beard in place with the other, was the worst fake Santa Claus I've ever seen in my life!!!

I'm not kidding, he looked so fake that I remember thinking, even in my shock, just how willing some people are to try to make the illusion of Santa Claus work. Meanwhile, the crowd below became determined that the Santa on the fire truck should become aware of the Santa on the throne and vice versa.

Papa, seeing what was happening, immediately rose to the occasion by standing and waving to the other Santa who, of course, had to hold onto his beard when he waved back. The crowd simply went BERSERK!

Then, as the parade turned the corner and went on its way, the fans returned to where they had been sitting. At first, there seemed to be a slightly uncomfortable mood hovering over them, as if some were nervous that the spell Papa had worked so hard to weave might have been broken.

Sensing this, Papa stood up, spread his arms wide, and gave the mightiest "HO! HO! HO!" of his career. Turning to me, he said, "See, Mama, it's just like Elvis told us—no matter how good the impersonator is, folks will always prefer the original."

Later that evening, I heard from more than one parent that Papa had given them the exact handle they needed, on what might otherwise have been a sticky situation. It turned out later that the fire chief, who had thrown this last-minute parade together, was just full of the Christmas spirit and had been unaware that the city had an "Official Santa."

Here's hoping we receive all future Christmas memos from the home office. And, oh, by the way, we did take that special picture with the Korean family.

— DIVA CLAUS

In the immortal words of Paul Harvey, "And now for the rest of the story, from Santa himself."

I just read Diva Claus' story, and there's one thing she left out. On that first evening after we had completed our visit to the family's home, we were driving through the downtown area as the parade vehicles were returning to the fire station. It was an exceptionally warm evening and I had already shed my Santa's hat, coat, and boots. Mama, as always, remained in full costume and make-up until we got home.

Seeing the red fire trucks backing into the station up ahead, Mama suddenly said she had an idea. She had me pull over to the curb a couple of doors down from the station. She checked herself in the mirror, then got out and walked up to the big entrance and then around the first fire truck to where the firefighters were helping Santa and the other celebrities down off the hook-and-ladder truck.

Then, in her most piercing DIVA CLAUS falsetto, she burst into the little knot of folks standing there, pointed, and then cried out, "YOO-HOO!!! SANTA!!! THERE YOU ARE . . . you naughty little boy!!! JUST WHEN were you planning, on coming back for me, HMMMMM?!?!?!"

The shock on the now beardless Santa was "PRICE-LESS." His wife was a little slow on the uptake and for a second, he was really in BIG trouble.

Mama then broke character and said, "Just kidding. My husband and I were forced to hide on the floorboards of our own car a little while ago because of you guys, and I just wanted to get even . . . MERRY CHRISTMAS."

At that exact moment, I pulled the sleigh up next to her and with a big smile on her face she stepped in. We drove away to ringing peals of laughter coming from the firefighters standing around their beardless Santa. As I looked back, I saw the poor guy trying to explain all this to his wife.

— SANTA RIC

SANTA TRIVIA: Santa Claus is now installing both Sirius and XM satellite radio in his sleigh. He wants to listen to Christmas music all night long.

Jeffrey's Present

It was while ringing the bell for the Salvation Army that I was offered my first job as a "real" Santa Claus. It was a cold December night when a lady stopped by my kettle and said, "You are the best looking Santa Claus I have ever seen." I thanked her and told her I appreciated her compliment.

She then asked if I made Santa calls on companies or if I did private parties. I told her I had not done that but I certainly would like to. As the result of that chance meeting, Phyllis Hendrix of Hendrix Batting Company became my first Santa client and has since become a dear friend. I enjoy visiting with her employees every year. I have seen many of the children grow up right before my eyes.

My visit, a few years ago, was especially memorable. I arrived early, so I decided to have dinner with everyone. As I walked in, I saw a little boy at the buffet getting only shredded cheese on his plate.

I asked if I could help, so I began small talk with him, asking if he liked cheese and if that was all he was going to eat. He told me his name was Jeffrey and he invited me to sit at his table with his family. When I agreed, he escorted me to the head of the table, and then took me back to the serving line where he dished out the food for me, describing how tasty it all was. He told me the green beans were good for me, but he didn't like them.

After escorting me back to the table, Jeffrey politely helped me off with my coat and placed it over the back of my chair like a little valet. I took my gloves off while he held my chair for me to sit down.

As we sat at the dinner table together, he asked me all sorts of questions about my reindeer, the North Pole, Mrs. Claus, and how I got there. He asked so many questions that his mother finally said, "Jeffrey, let Santa finish his dinner."

After a wonderful meal topped off with a piece of pumpkin pie with real whipped cream, Jeffrey helped me put my jacket, my gloves, and my cap back on. Then he led me to my chair next to a big beautiful Christmas tree. As he helped me get situated, all of the children came crowding around us.

Jeffrey asked me if he could be first, and I told him I didn't know whose present was whose and he would have to wait his turn as I called out the names. However, I told him he could be Santa's special helper since he knew all the children and could help me find them to listen to their Christmas list and then give them their gifts.

So one by one I called the children up to receive their present from Santa. Young children as well as older ones were delighted as they sat on Santa's knee and told him what they wanted for Christmas. Then, as Santa handed them their present, they would gleefully unwrap their gift to take home with them. There must have been twenty-five children.

I could tell that Jeffrey was getting a little nervous that there might not be a present for him, but he remained very patient. He would offer me a drink of water from time to time and would carefully put the glass on the table next to my chair. Each time another child's name was called he would enthusiastically announce their name to the crowd.

Finally, there was only one present left and Jeffrey looked concerned that the package might not be for him. I slowly picked it up, looked all over for his name, and then I found it. I was beginning to wonder what in the world I would say if it was not for him.

As I had done with each child, I asked Jeffrey what he would like Santa to bring him for Christmas. He told me that all he wanted was a fire truck. We began to talk about all of the fire trucks we have at Santa's Village at the North Pole, and I asked him which specific kind he wanted.

"I want a remote control fire truck with a ladder that goes up and down," he replied. I told him I would see what I could do, and thanked him for being such a great helper. He then slid off my lap so he could open his present.

As he began to tear the wrappings from the package that was nearly as big as he was, what should appear but the biggest, shiniest remote control fire truck I have ever seen! Jeffrey squealed with delight. Running back to me, he threw his arms around my neck, thanked me, and said, "You did it! You brought me just what I wanted! You knew all the time! Thank you, thank you, thank you!" To tell the truth, I was as surprised and delighted as he was!

What a wonderful gift that was for me, because you see, I don't believe in coincidences. My role as Santa Claus was authenticated in my own heart as I believe God quickly wrapped that last package to include the exact toy the last child had requested.

I believe that God led me to Jeffrey that night because He knew what a special little fellow he was—and on that night, Jeffrey needed a sign, a reason, to believe in Santa Claus—and so did Santa!

— SANTA CLIFF

SANTA BULLETIN: When Santa starts down your chimney, he presses his finger on the right side of his nose and then nods, which puts the fire out and shrinks him to the size of your chimney. When he steps out of your fireplace, he presses his finger on the left side of his nose, and nods again. He then expands back to his rather large size. Upon leaving your home, he simply reverses the process.

Questions?
Questions?
Questions?

I was asked to appear at the annual Cub Scout Christmas meeting and party. This event was held in a church, and I arrived a little early and was ushered into a hallway to await my entrance. Lining the hallway were several old wooden pews, and I sat down to wait for my cue.

With me in the hallway on one pew, was a father and his eleven-year-old daughter; and on another pew a young mother holding a blond-haired, cute as can be, three-year-old. This young boy looked at me with the fear we Santas have seen on many children's faces. I didn't make any quick moves and I was very deliberate with all my gestures.

With the encouragement of his mother, the young lad was soon warming up to Santa and was showing a few smiles on that cute face. In a little while, he became very brave and asked his mother to put him down.

With every moment, his courage grew and he did a little walk in circles getting ever closer to me. Much to his mother's amazement, he got closer and closer while asking me, "Where are your reindeer?" "Is it always cold at the North Pole?" and "Do you have an iPod on your sleigh?"

Now the little fellow was standing right in front of me. I bent over so we were at eye level, and I waited for his next question. He paused for a minute and then looked down at his little boots and said, "I've got boots and you've got boots." I said, "Yes, and your boots are shinny, too." He then looked me square in the eye, and pointing his finger, in a voice that seemed amplified, he said, "I've got a penis; does Santa have a penis?"

The father with his daughter nearly fell off the bench laughing while the mother scooped up the little boy faster than lightning. Her face was redder than my suit and she was apologizing nonstop. I was still laughing and I'm sure that happy tears were running down my face.

When things calmed down, the mother explained that they were potty training the young man and, thus, his fixation with the male anatomy. She was worried that I would think badly of her, but I assured her that his remark was a classic, which she will remind him of for many Christmases to come.

I will add that she did have a hard time looking directly at me the rest of the evening.

— SANTA LOU

"Pere Noel"

"Pere Noel" is the French Father Christmas. He dresses in a long robe, which may vary in color, rather than the more familiar red and white suit seen in the United States. He is generally riding a horse or walking his Christmas rounds because of the lack of snow.

He visits good French children during the holiday season, which runs from December 6 through January 6. He leaves gifts of candy and fruit in their stockings or shoes. A companion, "Pere Fouetiard," (The Punisher) accompanies him and leaves wood switches or lumps of coal for those children who have not been so good.

Many think of Santa Claus (Pere Noel) as a pagan figure, but the reality is quiet different. Santa (Pere) is the modern embodiment of a legend built around a real person—St. Nicholas—a true man of God who was a religious leader in a small town in Turkey many hundreds of years ago.

He emulated the unconditional love of Jesus and his generosity was so admired and appreciated that reports of his work were told throughout Europe. Over the years, his name has been translated into many languages.

— PERE NOEL ROBERT

Father Christmas

One holiday season I was a volunteer Father Christmas at a WinterFest, when a young couple with a preschool daughter and a little baby boy were strolling through the festival. The little girl spotted the Santa Claus House and stopped to look in.

I waved and her parents tried to entice her to enter for a visit with Santa, but the child stayed outside and the family continued on their way. Several minutes later, they again passed the entrance of the Santa House and once more the child looked in. Again, she refused to come in, despite a wave from Santa and urging from mom and dad.

Less than five minutes later, they walked by the House again. This time the four-year-old little angel came straight for me and threw her arms around my neck. She immediately began telling me all about herself and all about what she wanted for Christmas. Her parents followed her with looks of total amazement on their faces.

Once she had finished her visit and pictures were taken, she left with her mother and baby brother, talking and smiling all the way out. Her father stayed behind and related that the family had been to several shopping malls and the child simply refused to go anywhere near Santa's area.

Whenever the family tried to encourage her so they could get her picture with Santa Claus, their efforts were rewarded by crying and by a hasty retreat.

It turned out the family owned several Father Christmas figures dressed in traditional European robes rather than in Santa's more familiar red suit. After seeing me three times from afar, in her mind, my Father Christmas look was like the real figures she had at home. She knew that I was Santa and she felt safe talking and sharing her wish list with me.

The family returned to visit with me three more times over the course of the festival. The young girl kept insisting to her parents that she knew the Santa at the WinterFest was real because I looked just like the Santa figures she had at home.

— PERE NOEL ROBERT

A True Christmas

My Christmas holiday plans were set. I was heading off on my first trip to Tanzania, Africa, to work with a charity called Right To Play that uses sport and play to encourage healthy child development to build safer and stronger communities. In the back of my mind, in my own way, I would be a Santa Claus in Tanzania.

With one phone call, all of my plans came to a crushing halt. On the other end of the line, my mother was telling me she had been diagnosed with a very aggressive breast cancer. Cancer? That was something that happened to other families. Not mine!

Once I finally came to terms with the reality, I knew there was no question that I would travel back to my parents' home outside of Boston to support my mom. I wanted to be there for the surgery to remove her malignant lump and the start of her chemotherapy.

Then, following surgery, we discovered more bad news. The cancer had spread to her lymph nodes. I figured I could basically write off any Christmas joy that year.

I had decided not to travel to Africa so I could stay and assist my mother in her recovery. But she simply would not hear of it. She encouraged me to go and help the children who were in greater need and then come back and share my experiences of hope with her.

Once in Tanzania, I was filled with inspiration as I saw how the power of sport brought these children new expectations and dreams. Children who had a mere life expectancy of only forty-five years were finding ways to enjoy what little they had and were living each day to its fullest. Despite worries about my mother, I couldn't help but end each day with a smile.

When I returned home, I found my mother was ignited with that same zest for life that the children had. Sometimes life's greatest adversities can shake us hard enough to realize and value what we actually have.

Two weeks later I awoke in my same childhood bed, where I had always anticipated our Christmas tree and all its presents. But on this Christmas morning my eyes were suddenly opened to what Christmas truly meant. The joy I felt that day even surmounted the elation of finding a shiny red bike, so many years ago, next to the tree.

The experience with my mother and the children of Africa changed my attitude and appreciation, not only for Christmas day, but for all the days in between. The belief in Santa is the belief in giving, and nothing can compare with the gift of time with my family where I grew up and the gift of time with my family of children in Tanzania.

— Ms. NIKKI CLAUS

Charlie Jones

Santa Bear

Last year Mrs. Claus and I did many store appearances and as always, we gave a stuffed animal to each child after their visit with Santa Claus. Mrs. Claus works very closely with a local charity organization and is able to purchase, at a fraction of their cost, stuffed animals they have not sold at their charity store.

She then cleans each and every one, whether they need it or not, and puts a Christmas ribbon around them with a tag that has my picture and reads "Especially for you, From Santa." Mrs. Claus starts acquiring these stuffed animals every fall and by December, she always has at least 1,000.

This day, we were appearing at a local Food Festival to kickoff the Christmas season. A very long line had formed with children and their parents waiting for their turn to tell Santa they had been good and what they wanted for Christmas. Mrs. Claus was there selecting just the "right" stuffed animal for each child, which she presented with a hug right after their visit with Santa Claus.

A little girl we knew, named Timberly, came to sit on Santa's knee. She told me what she wanted for Christmas and that she had been a good girl. Then Mrs. Claus reached into her special bag for a little brown Teddy Bear, and gave it to her with a big hug.

Timberly was six years old and her eyes widened, her mouth fell open, and she grasped the bear, hugging it to her chest. Her grandmother read the tag to her, "Especially for you, From Santa." Her mouth dropped open again and she ran back and gave me a big hug and said, "I love you so much!" I replied, "I love you, too. And I hope you enjoy your Santa Bear."

Over the next few weeks, whenever we saw Timberly's grandmother, she told us that Timberly took that bear everywhere with her. She took it to school, to church, and she wouldn't even go to bed without her Santa Bear. Her grandmother said she had never loved any stuffed animal as much as this one and it was her constant companion.

We had an early appearance one morning and were getting ready, when the phone rang. It was Timberly's grandmother screaming into the phone. This was an emergency call and she had to yell into the phone because Timberly was crying so loudly, and she had been crying most of the night.

It seems when she got ready for bed last night, she went to get her Santa Bear out of her backpack and he was GONE! The child started searching all over the house for Santa Bear, to no avail. The more she searched, the more hysterical she became.

The Santa Bear was nowhere to be found and Timberly was totally heartbroken and beside herself with grief over the loss. Her grandmother wanted to know if we might have another little brown bear in our "stash" that could work as a substitute and bring some consolation to

Timberly. Realizing this was a true emergency, Mrs. Claus told her we'd take a look and call her back.

Through a true miracle, down in the bottom of one of Santa's bags was a little brown bear that looked as close to the original as one could get! We called her grandmother right back and told her we found one that might just do the trick. We would bring it by her house on the way to our appearance and Santa himself would present it to Timberly.

We did just that and when Timberly answered the door and saw Santa standing there, she gave that big wide-eyed look and her mouth formed a large smile. Santa told her he had heard about her misfortune in misplacing her Santa Bear and, because it was such a special bear, he just happened to have a brother. He asked if she would like to have it to comfort her while she continued to look for her Santa Bear?

"Oh yes, I sure would, and I'll take REAL good care of him."

I handed her the bear and she clutched it to her chest, and I saw a little tear of joy slide down the side of her face, as Timberly's heart touched ours. Her big beautiful eyes looked so lovingly at that little plain brown bear that I now knew why Mrs. Claus went to all that trouble to prepare those special stuffed animals for their new little owners.

— SANTA CHARLIE and MRS. CLAUS

Santa's Red Coat

I was working at a shopping mall one Christmas and the photographer wanted the area to have a North Pole Santa's Workshop feel. He wanted Santa in a long-sleeve festive shirt, red suspenders and sandals, rather than the red coat and black boot look.

I went along with the shirt and red suspenders, just as long as my red coat was nearby on a big hook. However, I did nix the sandals. We settled for a traditional Santa's Workshop, and I wore big black boots for photos with the kids.

We found that some of the kids, and even some of the families, had a tough time with Santa not wearing his red coat. However, there were others who thought the Workshop look was a nice change.

Toward the end of one busy day, I noticed this six-year-old little girl, with her mother, quietly standing in line for her visit with Santa. She had been watching me for several minutes as she waited her turn. When she and her mother stepped into the Workshop, the first thing the little girl said was, "You should be wearing your red coat."

I took my big red coat off its hook and asked this little girl if she would help Santa. Not only did she help me into my coat, she made sure my belt was straight and that all the little bells were visible.

Then I bent over so she could lift my beard to make sure my collar looked just right. You could tell she was so proud to help Santa get properly dressed, and that she was excited with her Christmas visit.

A few days later, the little girl's mother wrote a letter to the editor of the local paper about their visit. She wrote about how her daughter talked all the time about helping Santa and how that memory will last her for a lifetime.

A lot of nice people in that community cut out the letter from the paper and brought it to me. I have always treasured it and even today, I carry a copy in my wallet.

Those kinds of memories are not limited to little girls.

— SANTA JOE

SANTA BULLETIN: Santa loves all food, with one exception: He refuses to eat a venison (reindeer) burger.

The Midnight Visit

It was December and I received a call from a father who was in the process of getting a divorce and had joint custody of twin eight-year-old girls. While the twins were with their mother, she was telling them there was no Santa Claus. However, the father desperately wanted them to continue to believe. He had a plan and the following is what happened on that Christmas Eve.

At about ten o'clock that evening, the twins laid down on the two couches that were in the living room of their father's apartment. Also in that room was a beautifully decorated Christmas tree with absolutely nothing under it.

The girls, with blankets and pillows, were being bedded down for the night but not until they had left some milk and cookies for Santa. You see, one of the girls trusted their father, so she still believed in Santa. The other girl, swayed by her mother, was very doubtful there could be a Santa. The girls finally drifted off, and the scene was set.

Around midnight, dressed as Santa, I entered the apartment through a prearranged back door. Prior to this, while the girls were asleep, their father had filled the empty space under the tree with beautifully wrapped Christmas presents. I quietly walked in beside the tree, took a big bite out of one of the cookies, and followed that with a large swallow of milk.

Now my job was to make just enough noise that the girls would awaken and suddenly find Santa in his final motion of delivering the gifts wrapped by the elves at the North Pole. They were sound asleep. They were *really* sound asleep. I finally knocked over a chair. They opened their eyes and sat up in amazement.

Santa (me) said, "Oh, goodness, you caught me. I must have made too much noise. I didn't mean to wake you. I have to go. I have more deliveries to make." Then I rushed through the kitchen and just as I went out the back door, I heard one of the girls tell the other, "See, I told you Mom was wrong. There *is* a Santa Claus."

— SANTA JOE

SANTA'S POEM:
Christmas is more than a tree and a meal,
Christmas is a heart and a touch and a feel,
Christmas without a doubt, is the biggest, BIG DEAL.

Wheels of Hope

I have been a Santa for thirty-five years and while there have been a few memories that cause me to cringe when I think about them, such as slipping on the ice and falling or mistakenly calling a mother a grandmother, there are many more that have affected me in such a way that can only be called life changing.

In the early '90s, I was happy to be entertaining children at a local mall. The festive decorations were all in place and the Christmas shopping season was in full swing. A train had been brought in for the kids and it seemed as if each time I would ask someone what Santa could bring them this Christmas, the whistle on the train would blow and I would have to ask them to repeat their requests. This constant whistle, although it added to the experience for future locomotive engineers, was a source of irritation, and had the makings of a long night.

This was true until a grandmother approached me with her grandson, who had sandy hair and dark eyes. He was in a solid black wheelchair, and I could tell he was despondent. He looked at me with the weight of sadness pressing down on his shoulders in an all-encompassing crush. I said, "Hello, young man; what do you want from Santa?" He looked at me, with no glint of hope in his eyes, and answered, "I want to be normal."

I looked at his grandmother, and her eyes were welling with tears as she rubbed his hair lovingly. I looked back at this precious child, no more than twelve years old, wondering how Santa could fill him with any hope.

There aren't many times that something one of these children says to me causes me to struggle for an answer. But at that moment, I was instantly in contact with the "Spirit of Christmas" itself when I asked him if he liked motorcycles.

His eyes lit up, a smile crept on his face, and he looked at me apprehensively, wondering what I could possibly say about motorcycles. I then told him about a friend of mine who was a paraplegic. He, too, had an incredible love for motorcycles and wasn't going to let his challenge stop him from enjoying his favorite hobby.

His brother, seeing how this love gave him hope, designed a motorcycle with a sidecar, so he could wheel his wheelchair up onto the sidecar, and then have complete control of the motorcycle by using hand controls built into the sidecar.

At this point, the boy's eyes were shining like Rudolph's nose, and the excitement was all over his face. He wanted to know where he could get this kind of a motorcycle and sidecar. I told him to call the Harley Davidson dealership in town and they could set him up.

I looked up at his grandmother and she was misty-eyed again, but this time for a different reason. She had come to see Santa with her grandson, who had no hope and was mired in despair, and she was looking at this same young man who was now full of dreams and aspirations. We talked for a couple more minutes, they both said goodbye, and the grandmother rolled him away.

I never saw them again, but I have found myself wondering how they were doing and how he liked being able to ride around and be "normal."

The memories of talking with that young man almost fifteen years ago, seeing the change on his face, and thinking of him riding around, the wind blowing through his hair, his face gleaming with joy, always brings a huge smile to my face. I will always hope that he realized his dreams, as meeting him will stay with me for the rest of my life.

— SANTA DONALD
(As told to Tony Aveyard)

Joey

I work full-time for our county's Department of Family Services at its shelter for abused and neglected children. I am their resident Santa and remain in character all year with full white beard, a combination of red clothing, and a pocketful of candy or Santa stickers.

Recently, a sibling group of ten came into our care and one of the boys, whom I'll call "Joey" (not his real name), was especially taken with Santa. Joey was six years old and his nine brothers and sisters ranged in age from infant to teenager.

I make it a point to visit all the children in the facility, and some are very shy about approaching me. Joey was not. Whenever I visited his cottage, he would always talk to me about anything and everything that was on his mind.

He always had a hundred questions for and about Santa and his activities. Our conversation always started and ended with hugs for Santa. The attention he craved was more than just a need to overcome the neglect that had placed him in our shelter in the first place. Joey just loved Santa Claus.

When Joey came to the Administration building with our staff for counseling or medical appointments, and spotted me, he would break away from the staff member and run to give his "Santa" a big hug. He always received a big hug in return and usually a piece of candy or a Santa sticker. He never asked or begged for one. The only time he asked for candy was when he wanted to share it with his brothers and sisters. Once the hugs were exchanged, he would run back to the staff member and continue on his way, excitedly explaining that he had talked with Santa and Santa had given him a gift.

But it was Joey who blessed Santa with a gift. The gift was unconditional love and respect from a child who had not known real love in his young life, and yet could remain happy and upbeat, despite his circumstances.

This story ends happily – with a new beginning.

"Joey" and his brothers and sisters, all ten of them, were placed with a great foster family that was able to provide love and care for all of them and keep them together as their own family.

— PERE NOEL ROBERT
(A French Father Christmas)

Possum Creek Festival

For several years, my church held the Possum Creek Festival in late September on our sixty-acre campus to raise funds for missions and to connect with folks in the neighborhood. It was quite a large, well-attended fall festival and a major effort by our church. We typically had about 100 vendors and nearly 10,000 visitors.

Over the years, when a vendor needed more traffic, I would go there with my bucket of joy (I always used joy so I could say that) and make some great big bubbles—and here would come the kids.

I was already being recognized as Santa, so I decided to pull out all the stops. My dilemma was what to wear. I couldn't wear a Santa suit, not when the heat in September reaches the high eighties in North Central Florida.

A good friend embroidered a white polo shirt with a beautiful Santa and a large "ON VACATION," plus I bought red swimming trunks and a red cap. I was all set. In fact, one lady walked by and said, "You almost make the adults believe!" "Of course," I replied. "And well they should."

Once I was bent down making bubbles and a little boy squatted down so he could look under the bill of my cap into my eyes. He asked, "What's your name?" I replied, "Santa Claus." He peered under the brim again, "Why is that your name?" Now, that was an unexpected question. No answer. More bubbles, I still didn't have an answer.

I said, "What's your name?" I figured the best defense is a good offense. "Ian," was his reply. "Why is that your name?" No answer. More bubbles. I said, "Don't I look like Santa Claus?" Ian slowly nodded his head yes, followed by, "Uh huh," as the realization spread over his face.

You could almost see him thinking, Oh, what have I done! I've crossed Santa! After a few more bubbles, we said goodbye and with a smile and a wave, I said, "Be a good boy!" And I bet he will be, all the way to Christmas.

I took a break for lunch, even Santa's have to eat, and I sat down in one of the few empty chairs in the food tent. I found myself across from Ben, a little friend not quite three years old. He was thrilled to have lunch with Santa but he talked so fast I had trouble understanding him.

As we ate, he calmed down somewhat. Then, after a while, he got out of his chair and came to my side of the table. His mom said he wanted to tell me something. Then, completely serious and with absolute conviction, he looked me straight in the eye and said, "God is great!" Expecting three-year-old chatter, I was completely blown away. He had grasped the heart of most religions and offered it to me.

As Santa, we hear a lot of childish talk. But on occasion, we are offered wisdom far beyond the years or even comprehension of a small child. Such occasions are the affirmation from above that we, as Santas, are truly called to spread God's love.

— SANTA HUGH

T'was the night before Christmas,
And all through my room,
Not a creature was stirring,
Not even a broom.

I tried to sleep,
But kept watching the clock.
Was he really going to be here?
All I could hear was tick, tock.

Then before I knew it,
T'was barely the light of day.
The sound of the sleigh,
That deep voice, "Up, up, and away!"

Now I could close my eyes,
For all was well.
My secret was safe,
And I'll never tell.

"A God Moment"

I have been making a personal Santa visit to one particular family for many holidays. A few years ago, Abby, one of the youngest of the children there, came over to me. Her grandmother said, "Santa, Abby has a gift and would like for you give it to some other child this coming Christmas." As I turned back to Abby, with her cute two-year-old smile, she handed me a small, neatly wrapped box with a bow on top.

I looked up, with a surprised smile on my face, and her grandmother explained that in this gift box was Abby's precious "Binky" that she now wanted to give to another little girl so she could enjoy it, too.

I thought about how many people give gifts they can easily afford but to which they have no real attachment. This was a precious gift given by a child who would normally not want to part with it, but she was entrusting it to me. I promised Abby that I would pass her true Christmas gift on to another special little girl.

The next Christmas, when I again visited Abby (now three years old and without a new "Binky"), I was able to tell her that her gift was greatly appreciated by another child. She responded with her cute happy smile and a bright Santa-like twinkle in her eyes.

For me, this was a "God Moment." He had called my attention to the preciousness of even the littlest gifts given at Christmas. I now look forward to a new, different, and special "God Moment" every year.

— SANTA RICH

SANTA BULLETIN: A young New Yorker named Thomas Nast, a cartoonist for *Harper's Weekly,* began creating sketches of Santa Claus during the Civil War. He portrayed him as jolly, plump, grandfatherly, and wearing a RED SUIT.

"Now I want you to meet my
friend, Pat Hart, who was
truly the Spirit of Christmas
to the men and women
who fought in Vietnam.
I can hear her now . . ."

Christmas Eve

During the 1960s, I was a young flight attendant for United Airlines and was privileged to be a part of the crew that flew our fighting men in and out of Vietnam. The flight I most remember involved the last leg, from Honolulu to Travis Air Force Base near San Francisco.

It was Christmas Eve and due to some technical glitches, we weren't to arrive until around midnight. This was one of those rough flights. These men had been fighting the Viet Cong early that morning, and then had rush orders to clear out in a hurry. They were told to grab what they could and head for the airstrip at Bien Hoa.

They were tired, grubby, and had been sitting on the plane for eighteen hours. Some were even nursing minor injuries. I suspect others had worse wounds they didn't want to call attention to once they heard they were headed back to "the world," which is what they called anyplace outside Vietnam.

When fighting in a Vietnam jungle, there's a tendency to forget what day it is. It just doesn't matter. What matters is, it's today, and you're alive.

So, just as a reminder, we decorated the cabin the best we could with red and green ornaments, lots of silver icicles and, of course, mistletoe. To give you an idea of how beat these men were, not one of our quite attractive stewardesses was asked for a kiss under the mistletoe.

When the Captain finally came on the P.A. and announced an anticipated arrival in the U.S.A. in forty-five minutes, there was an immediate stirring, followed by a mad rush for the "blue rooms." (That's what we called our restrooms.) Grubby fatigues suddenly looked crisp and new. Boots were dusted and shined.

Then one young Marine stepped out of a blue room and began to quietly sing, "I'll Be Home for Christmas." Almost the whole plane joined in. He continued to lead us in one carol after another: "Silent Night," "The First Noel," "Joy to the World." Oh, he had such a beautiful voice.

By the time the seat belt sign came on, we were into a hilarious rendition of "The Twelve Days of Christmas," complete with sound effects, geese, drummers, and maids.

As they deplaned down the stairs, every man wished us a warm "Merry Christmas" before stepping back into "the world." At that very moment, the clouds parted and "the world" was drenched at that midnight hour in the light of a beautiful full moon.

As I stood in the doorway of that plane and watched them all cross the tarmac, with their shadows reaching out to heaven, all I could think of was, "Merry Christmas to all and to all a good night."

— Ms. PAT CLAUS

THE FOUR STAGES OF SANTA CLAUS:
1. You believe in Santa.
2. You don't believe in Santa.
3. You ARE Santa.
4. You look like Santa.

Merry
Christmas!

Contributing Santas and Mrs. Clauses

(Alphabetical Order)

Tony Aveyard

Arthur Bahl

Robert Callet

Warren Clement

Dean Curtis

Jeff Curtis

Jerry Ellsworth

Ric Erwin

Victoria Erwin

Jeff Germann

Jac Grimes

Lowell Hendrickson

John Johnson

Michelle Johnson

Lou Knezevich

Karl Koebke

Martin S.C. Lebowitz

Barbara McDaniel

Jerry McDaniel

Hugh McDowell

Ed Mechenbier

Joe Moore

Joe Mystic

Joe Neves

Merlin Olsen

Bud Orrin

Nina Orrin

Dale Parris

Trish Parris

Rich Sagan

Joe Shurman, MD

Charlie Smith

Cliff Snider

Dave Speer

Nikki Stone

Michael Sypherd

Charlie Thomas

Cindy Thomas

Tom Tumminello

Donald Wesley

About the Author

Charlie Jones is the *New York Times* bestselling author of *What Makes Winners Win.* He has written nine other books: *Christmas Memories; A Christmas To Remember; Confessions of a Gate Crasher;* and co-authored with Kim Doren, *You Go Girl; Be The Ball; Game Set Match; That's Outside My Boat; If Winning Were Easy;* and *Heaven Can Wait—Surviving Cancer.* He was a network sportscaster with NBC and ABC for forty years and has been inducted in the Pro Football Hall of Fame. In addition, he broadcast fifty College Football Bowl Games, three Olympic Games, and traveled more than five million miles broadcasting thirty-two different sports in forty-one states and twenty-five foreign countries. An undergraduate at the University of Southern California, he graduated with a JD degree from the University of Arkansas Law School, where he has received their Distinguished Alumnus Award and has been honored as their Commencement Speaker. Charlie resides in beautiful La Jolla, California.